Copyright © 2015 by Bojana Lambrou. 714191

ISBN: Softcover 978-1-5144-0611-3
Hardcover 978-1-5144-0612-0
EBook 978-1-5144-0610-6

All rights reserved. No part of this book may be reproduced or transmitted in any form or by any means, electronic or mechanical, including photocopying, recording, or by any information storage and retrieval system, without permission in writing from the copyright owner.

This is a work of fiction. Names, characters, places and incidents either are the product of the author's imagination or are used fictitiously, and any resemblance to any actual persons, living or dead, events, or locales is entirely coincidental.

Print information available on the last page

Printed in the United States of America by
BookMasters, Inc
Ashland OH
December 2015

Rev. date: 12/10/2015

To order additional copies of this book, contact:
Xlibris
1-888-795-4274
www.Xlibris.com
Orders@Xlibris.com

# BOJANA LAMBROU

Illustrated By Lyle Jakosalem

Loli wants to visit
A beautiful, new place,
"Let's go to Paris,
The capital of France!"

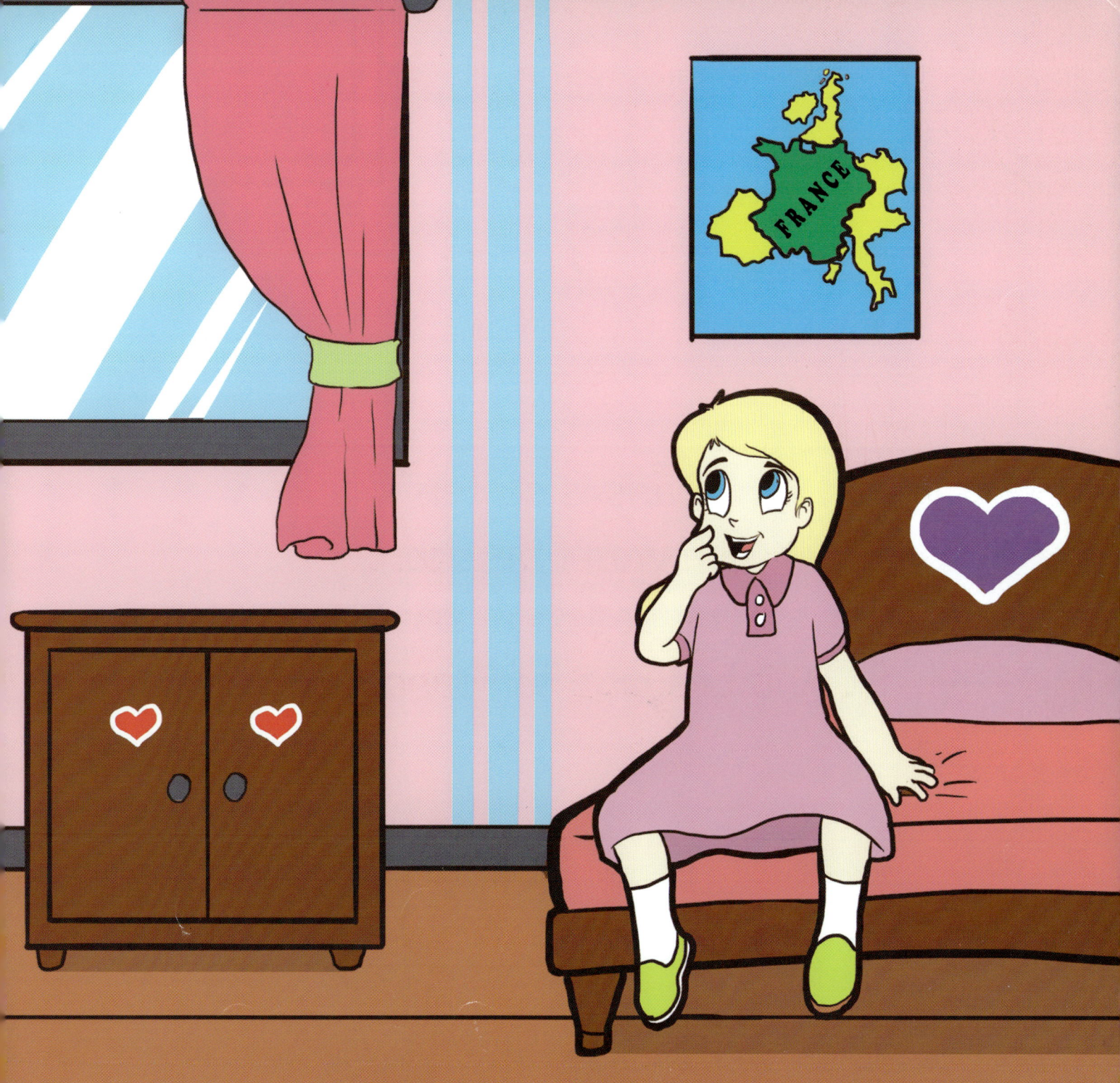

Paris is so far,
Trip won't be short,
She got on a plane
And brought her passport.

Paris is confusing,
Loli needs a ride,
Here comes Pierre,
Her private tour guide.

Pierre explained everything
To keep her in the loop,
They went to a restaurant
And ate french onion soup.

Pierre said she must try
the famous french cheese.
Loli was excited,
"Can I have some, please?"

French deserts are yummy
Pierre loves crème brûlée,
but Loli's favorite
Is chocolate soufflé.

Many ways to see Paris,
So lucky we can choose,
"Let's go to Seine River
And get on a cruise!"

"What's that gorgeous building?
Let's play a guessing game!"
Loli didn't know
It's Cathedral Notre Dame

It was time for Louvre
Best museum of all
Famous painting of Mona Lisa
Is there on the wall.

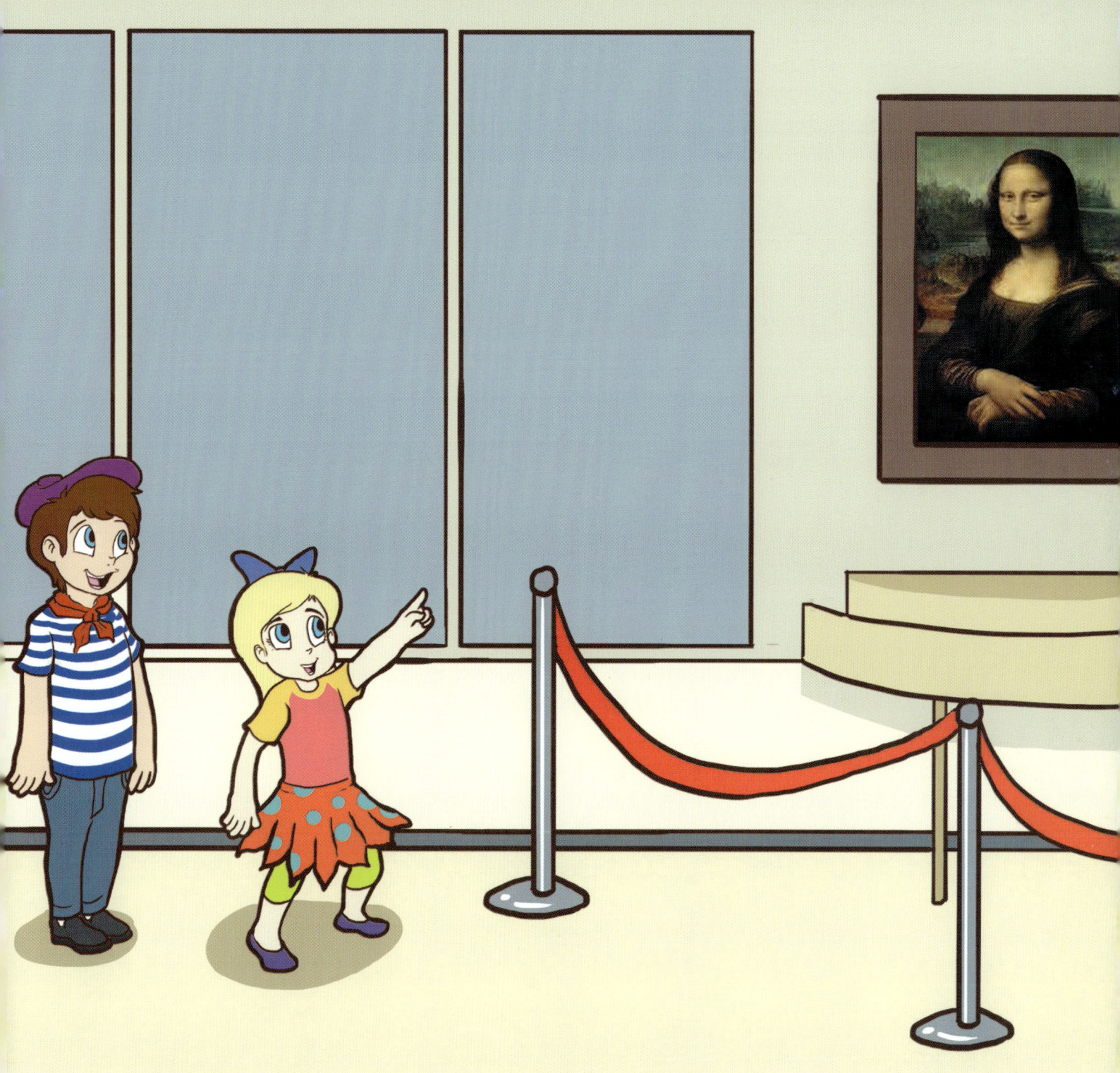

They went to Champs-Élysées
But Loli wanted more
She glanced at the window
Of a beautiful store

Loli thought,
"I can look French, I bet!
All I need is a beret,
the famous french hat."

There is more to see
You have to have faith.
Arch of Triumph, farther down,
Looks just like a gate.

It was getting late
They had just an hour
They decided to go to
See the Eiffel Tower.

The tower looks amazing
Loli had a blast,
"It's great when you leave
The best for last."

Loli got a puppy,
French poodle, Bercy.
Now, instead of "thanks"
She only says *merci*.

On the way back home,
She ate french raspberries,
"I can't wait," Loli said,
"To come back to Paris!"